TO Kyle + Tyler

may the soul of love

fill you with Joy this day

and always

          with love,

          uncle Ronnie

Apples & Oranges

Apples & Oranges

Ron Martin

Rochdale, Massachusetts

ISBN: 978-1-4907-5227-3 (sc)
ISBN: 978-1-4907-5228-0 (hc)
ISBN: 978-1-4907-5229-7 (e)

Library of Congress Control Number: 2014922109

Trafford rev. 01/06/2015

 www.trafford.com
North America & international
toll-free: 1 888 232 4444 (USA & Canada)
fax: 812 355 4082

To my dear friend Berta
who taught me how to live again

and

to my children,
Joel, Laura, and Cheryl

For God so loved the world that He gave His one and only Son, that whoever believes in Him shall not perish but have eternal life.

John 3: 16

Apples and Oranges

id you ever think that apples and oranges could lead you to Christ? There is a secret to all of this. The "apple" represents the Garden of Eden and the "orange," well, I'll have to let you in on this a little later in the story.

Well the garden was spectacular, flowers and trees and animals of every kind with an abundance of God's special treasures. He had prepared a home for all of His creatures, but especially for His own kind, the

ones who were created in His own image,
humans, men and women and children who
would eventually populate the universe. It
was paradise, and God was in control.

There was one stipulation; and that was to
never eat from the Tree of Knowledge
because that Tree was so bad that if you just
ate one fruit from it, you were certainly
going to die. There was no doubt about it
and God knew it. And He said to woman
and man, do not eat that fruit but to eat
only the fruit that He prepared for His
children because it was good, and there was
always an abundance of it.

The Garden of Eden was special. It was alive
with splendor, beauty beyond compare. Yet
there was one thing there that was not, and
that was the "Tree of Knowledge." The Tree

of Knowledge was ugly beyond description. It was hideous, outrageous, distasteful and incredibly detestable and God hoped that the woman and the man would find this tree the same as He saw it. And He placed on this tree "apples," not many, only two. And He said, "If you eat these two fruit you will surely die."

Who would ever question God, because He was always right and He knew best how to protect his children? God knew beyond a shadow of any doubt that as soon as He said, "Don't," they would say, "why not?" At least to themselves anyway. How could two apples make anyone die? It didn't seem possible.

So, they would go about their business each and every day and they were faithful to God in being obedient to him, until one day, while they were about their work, Eve ran across a snake. Now, the snake was very cunning. He was intelligent beyond compare. And the snake said to Eve, "What do you think of this tree, the tree of knowledge?" "It is one of the most beautiful trees in the Garden." Eve had remembered what God had spoke of that tree, and so she decided not to listen to that snake, at least for the time being.

And time would go on. One day led to another and then one day, while Eve was about her business, she met up with that cunning snake again. And again he would tell her about the tree. He told her that the fruit from this tree would make her brilliant beyond anything she could ever imagine. And so she thought of how that would make her like her Father, her Dad, her God in heaven.

See, her Father was God, and she felt, if she was as smart as God, how would that cause her to die? And so she was interested in what the snake had to offer. She would sit and listen to that snake whenever she got the chance.

She pondered in her heart what would it be like to be so smart that she would have the galaxy eating out of her own hand. For that must be what it was like to be God, to have total control, to be in charge, and to be the ruler of the universe.

She would go to the Tree and she would smell the apple that hung from the limb. It was small and gray. It didn't have anything about it that she desired. The only thing that attracted her to that tree was the snake.

Eve would sit thinking, could I just take one bite, only one small itty-bitty bite? Who would know? Eve was tempted, and she didn't even know it, but God knew, because He created that tree and the snake, with its wickedness, also. God knew that Eve would be the first to bow down to the temptation of sin because Eve was the weaker of the two.

The day of the departure from Eden was creeping up on Adam and Eve and they did not even know it. God had big plans; He was going to send them on a journey into the real world, the world of evil and destruction. He wanted them to know what it was like being without His love and being totally on their own. He knew that Eve would eat that apple even before He planted that tree, because our God is in control of all things, even the desires of the flesh.

God does not do the tempting, but he is in charge of the tempter and that temper's name is Lucifer. Lucifer was a fallen angel. He was created by God to shine as bright as the stars and that is why his name was called the "Morning Star." God was happy with Lucifer and he gave Lucifer charge of all of His possessions. God thought that Lucifer could be trusted, and he was for a time until he got to big for his own britches. See Lucifer got proud. He never wanted to bow down to any one. He felt that if he was in control of all of God's possessions, then why shouldn't he have them totally for himself? He forgot how powerful God really was.

Lucifer started to betray God. He would play tricks on him up in heaven. What seemed like a joke to Lucifer was very serious business to God. God didn't like Lucifer's

attitude, and He told him if he continued to
be bad he would be punished and he was
good for a time until he got another plan
and that plan was to deceive God. He was
going to tempt man into doing Sin. His plan
was to tempt Eve into eating that apple from
the Tree of Knowledge and that is what he
planned to do.

Lucifer turned himself into a snake. He
became the lowest of the low and he was
determined to get even with God. He
would talk with that woman whenever he
got the chance. He knew it was only a
matter of time before he would hook her
like a fish and reel her in. He was con-
stantly at her back, pushing her to her
limit. Then, finally she broke down. Her
thoughts of being like her Father were too
much to ignore.

"What must it be like to be like God," she would ponder. "To have everything at your command, I mean even the ocean waves stop at his command?"

What seemed like good to Eve was so, so bad with God, because God knew what it was like to be on top. It was such a lonely place. God knew the moment that Eve ate that apple she would want everything for herself. She wouldn't want to serve God any more but to be served by God. And, *isn't that how many Christians are today?* They think that God should bow down to their every whim. God knows that we all have needs, and He always provides for His children in His own good timing, but when you demand from Him, what He is not prepared to give, He gets angry. And that is how God felt with the apple.

He didn't want Eve to know what was good and bad, because all that she knew was good. He knew that as soon as she ate the apple that sin would enter her spirit, and that she would have to be driven away from paradise because in paradise there is no room for sin, because it is a holy place, set aside by God, to have fellowship with His children.

Eve was the first to bite the apple and then she gave the second apple to Adam. She told Adam that the apple was good and that she could now see with the eyes of the Lord. Everything became clear to her; she saw things like she never saw before, and she told Adam it is good. Adam was not willing to eat that apple that Eve had given to him. He was convinced that God was right and that he would certainly die if he ate of it. But Eve was persistent. She would tell Adam about the galaxies and planets and how each planet circled around the sun. She would teach him right from wrong and she also told Adam that he would also be like God in every way. Now how could that cause death? She would teach Adam about the birds and the bees, and she was determined to have Adam be like her, because she now knew what it was like to be like God.

Eve was enlightened she had free will. She could do as she pleased, and God knew it. He knew it because as you know God loves us so much that he even allows us to choose to be disobedient to him, because He knows that is the only way that you will ever learn that He is right. God knew that as soon as Eve bit that apple that she would know that

God would be angry with her. God is in control and don't you forget it.

Eve was not alone in that garden; she had Adam with her. And so she wanted him to have what she had also. She felt that if she could convince Adam that the apple was good, and then God would see also that He was wrong.

Eve would ponder at the thoughts of God, "Did he really mean not to eat that apple or did He say, 'don't eat that apple,' (knowing as soon as he said it that she would partake of it)"? Eve's only thought was the apple was so good and she wanted Adam to be as brilliant as she was. She would coach Adam in math, she would talk about arithmetic and spelling and the dissecting of animals, the functions of the human body, the liver and kidneys and especially the heart. The heart, as she saw it, was good, because it is warm and lovable. But God saw it as evil because it can deceive the mind of men and that is where Eve found Adam's weakness. She found his weakest link. She would also lure Adam in as Lucifer had done to her. She was determined and it was only a matter of time.

The garden where Adam and Eve lived was now beginning to change. It was not Heaven or paradise any longer, because the wages of sin are death and that sin which began in paradise is now dominating the world today.

People sin all the time, and we have all become tolerant of it. You know what is bad and good, but you allow bad to take over your lives. Why do you suppose that is? I think it is the heart that has deceived you, like Eve wanting to be like God. It was the heart that caused her to fall to the temptation of sin.

Adam had given up. He fought the good fight but the desires of the flesh were too much to handle. It was the thought of woman being dominant over him that had caused his great fall. So he took that apple in his hand and he ate it like there was no tomorrow and when he did, it was just like Eve had said it would be. He was brilliant, smarter than any animal in the forest. He could tell the time of the day and the season of the year, he also could tell right from wrong and he now knew why God told him not to eat that apple, because now he knew he would have to leave that garden, the paradise that God prepares for all His children. Adam and Eve would now have to leave their Father's home because God is so strict that He would not hesitate to punish His children, nor should we.

God knew that it was time for Adam and Eve to find out for themselves whether to be obedient to God or to be given over to their temptation and so He sent them both on their way. They were driven from paradise and not allowed back until they could prove to God that they knew He was right. Adam and Eve were sadden, they knew that God had done was only for their best interest, because God is always right and never wrong, and they were determined to get to the bottom of this. Adam and Eve would begin their journey through life and it was a lonely place without God's fellowship. Little did they know, God was opening every door and window for them. He would put the desires of His heart into Adam and Eve, and they didn't even know it.

God wishes everyone to want the desires of His heart, but not everyone is in tune with Him. It is only after you accept Jesus Christ as your Lord and Savior will God come into your life. And, that's the way it is with God.

Then how do you suppose God got into the heart and soul of Adam and Eve after they left the Garden of Eden? Well, God told Adam and Eve that the wages of sin are death and that's how he saw it. And nobody was going to get around that, not even His one and only son, Jesus.

Jesus was born, as you may well know, in a small village called Bethlehem. He grew up

as a child in Nazareth. His father was a
carpenter and Jesus loved to be with his dad
more than anything else in the world, even
better than going to church. Can you
believe that? His father was mighty as an ox.
He was stronger than any other man in
town. So strong that he would carry Jesus
with him wherever they would go. Jesus was
not like his dad, he was small and petite, not
a strong man at all. But he would walk tall
and he would carry a big stick with him
when he got to be a man. He would walk
from town to town. There was one thing on
his mind, and that was to be the King of
the Jews.

I often question why the Jews were so special
to Jesus when they were so disobedient to
God. Why do you suppose they were called
the Chosen Ones? I believe that the Jews

had a place in Jesus' heart, unlike any other
race. They were the ones who would nail
him to that cross. We all are responsible for
nailing Jesus to that cross because we all
have sinned and the wages of sin is death.
And that is why Jesus went to that cross in
the first place. But the Jews should have
known about Jesus.

Long before Jesus was born, there was Adam
and Eve who had left the Garden of Paradise. They, too, knew they needed a savior
way back then. And, that's how Adam and
Eve knew that God was watching over them.
Because they were saved already, they were
just waiting for the Messiah to come.

Adam and Eve had a child his name was
Cain. His name fit him well because Cain
was always on Adam's knee. Did you ever

hear of raising Cain? Well, that is how it was after Adam and Eve left Paradise. They had Cain and he was so naughty that they couldn't keep Cain from being bad. Whenever they turned around, Cain was up to something and always into mischief. Cain had a brother when he got a little older. His name was Abel. Abel loved to be good because he was Abel. Being good was simple for him because he listened to his father and he loved to obey.

Cain and Abel would always play together. They had no one else to play with so they made the best of it. The only problem was that Cain would get jealous of Abel because Abel would never tell a lie and he was so good that his parents would pay special attention to him. Cain would start to think of ways to get back at Abel. And finally he

knew just what to do. He was going to kill
Abel and tell his parents, "Abel was eaten
by lions."

God was watching all this from his throne in
Heaven and He was in complete control. He
allowed Abel to be killed by Cain because
that is the way it is with God. Who's to question His good judgment? God spoke down
to Cain. "Where is your brother Abel?" Cain
was surprised when he heard God's voice.
He thought that he was alone and when
God spoke, Cain trembled. Cain was so
scared he wept with fear. The Lord God
knows everything that goes on at all times
and all places. There is not a single thing
that He is not in control of and don't you
ever forget that. Cain was driven out of the
forest and never heard from ever again.

Adam had another son, his name was Seth
and Seth had sons as well. And the chain
continued until it came to Noah.

Now Noah was a mighty and holy man. He
was more righteous than any man who ever
lived at that time. And one day while Noah
was about his business, he was called upon
by the most high God. Now Noah was not
accustomed to being spoken to by God and
when he first heard Him speak, he trembled
with fear. Now God knew this would happen
and so He said to Noah "Fear not, it is your
Father in Heaven who speaks with you."
Noah settled down and he started to ponder
why God would want to have anything to do
with him, because he was only a carpenter
and did not have much of any intelligence
or anything like that he thought God would

desire. He did not know that his type of man is what God treasures most of all, because they are always going about the Lord's business.

Noah loved to spread the good news, and the news was the Savior's birth. The king would one day come back to this earth and rescue all who have been condemned to die because of sin. Noah was so much fun to be with. He would always be joyful and always on his best behavior.

He would minister to the children and to the older people as well. But his real passion was with the children because they were the ones who had a thirst for what Noah had to say.

One day, while Noah was about his business, God spoke again. And, this time He told

Noah that He wanted Noah to build an ark,
an ark so big that it would hold two animals
of every kind, a male and female, that
walked the earth and yes, two birds of every
kind, also.

Noah was determined to do what the Lord
had told him to do and so he started to
build the ark, without hesitation, with his
three sons and his wife as well. And, they did
make some progress. And people from town
would gather and watch as the great carpenter Noah was about his business construct-
ing the ark.

Noah had all the dimensions down on
paper. They were given to Noah, by God, far
in advance. Noah had to prepare his mind
for the job because to build an ark was no
easy task for anyone to do, especially in

those days because the only tools that Noah had were in that carpenter's box.

Noah would start his day early. Before the rooster crowed Noah would be about the Lords business, and he would stop only long enough to get a bite to eat. And yes, he was blessed with an abundance of food, because all the people of the town where Noah lived had a passion for the Lord as well, and they would help Noah and his family to construct the ark whenever they got the chance, and when they came they would always bring food with them and Noah and his family were blessed.

Time would go on and people lost interest in that ark because it was only an ark and there was no need for an ark where they lived because there was no water, only mist

that would drop down from heaven to water
the plants there. And so one by one the
people would start to question Noah and
ask him why the ark had to be built. Noah
was not sure why, he was just being obedient to God. He felt if God wanted him to
build an ark, he would build it and that
was that.

Do you believe God would want to wipe out
all of His children on this earth with a
flood? No way, God had hoped that He
could convince the people that there was
going to be a flood and then they would
repent because they would believe the end
had finally come. He wanted them to think
that Jesus was knocking on their door. See,
it was only a matter of time before the angel
of death would come and claim all of His
followers.

The angel was no angel at all. He was the
most disgusting beast that would ever live.
And that is how God had planned it. The
angel of death was in fact the angel that also
deceived Eve in the Garden of Eden.

Noah was now left to build that ark by himself, his children and his wife. They were his
only hope. He hoped that maybe one day
soon it would be finished. And the day that
he drove in that last nail, that very last nail,
it started to rain.

The King Is Coming

So it was in the days of Noah, so will it be when our Savior returns.

Just as Noah was putting the finishing touches on that ark the rain started to fall. Now Noah had never seen rain before this, and when the rain began to fall Noah couldn't believe his eyes. He was so amazed because it was all new to him but it was just like he imagined it would be. He started to see now why God was having him build an ark, an ark so big it would hold two animals of every kind, male and female, and yes, two birds of every kind as well. Noah knew as soon as the first drop of rain hit his forehead that the destroyer was about to do his business.

God told Noah in a dream about a great flood that was going to consume the whole planet and when that flood came that it would raise that ark that Noah had built and the ark would float away and never be seen or heard from again.

The ark that Noah had built was built so strong that it could withstand even the most mightiest of storms. Seas as high as forty feet over the top of the ark would come crashing down could not stop this ark because this ark was designed by God. He had designed every inch of it, and He knew that it would withstand the storm because He created the storm as well.

Now, Noah thought that the rain that was coming down would cause the people from town to stop from doing their evil deeds. Yes, they were not all holy and righteous as Noah was. They had become the lowest of the low in the short period of time since they had fellowship with Noah and his family building that ark. They had become vile, mean, ornery, despicable and outrageously ungodly. Their attitude was it was all for me and nobody else. And, they started to deceive people into doing the most sinful acts that any human being could do. They started to have sex with the opposite partner and with the same partners as well, male and female and male and male. And, when God saw this He became atrociously mad because He designed man in His own image. He never intended for man to have sexual relations with another man. And, that is why He was having Noah build that ark, because He was going to wipe out sin before it wiped out man.

Now Noah was in for a devastating disappointment. He thought that as soon as the people from the town saw the rain they would repent from doing their sinful acts before God but just the opposite happened. The people started to become more sinful.

Whatever is true, whatever is noble, whatever is right, whatever is pure, whatever is lovely, whatever is admirable, if anything is excellent or praiseworthy, think about such things.

Now, Noah had forgotten how tempting the devil Satan could be. He was in for a devastating surprise. He thought that the rain would cause the people to repent and when this did not happen Noah wept so hard that he could not stop, he was devastated. He wanted to have fellowship with the people from town but he could not, because if he did, he would also have to die because that's the way it is.

Noah had become righteous. He knew what is like to be holy in the sight of God. Noah knew because he wasn't always holy. It was the same with him before he started to walk with God. Yes, Noah was a sinful man and he had fallen short of the kingdom of God. Noah was to be condemned to die. And, then one night he saw the light. A light so

bright it caused his eyes to become translu-
cent. Now Noah would see with the eyes of
the Lord. He would now know that it was not
right to fool with Mother Nature and that is
when Noah began his walk with the Lord.

Noah's walk with the Lord was unique, it was
so amazing. And, when the people from the
town saw how much Noah had changed and
how happy he had become they wanted to
become happy also. And, they were so
intrigued by what Noah had to say.

Noah told the people from town that he had
seen a light, a light so bright that it blinded
him so that he had to stop what he was
doing. And, then he heard a voice. It was
the voice of a great heavenly being. It was
the Lord God, himself. The Lord had told
Noah to build an ark so big that it would

hold two animals of every kind, a male and female, that walked the face of the earth, and yes, two birds of every kind as well.

Noah did not know why he was to build the ark. He just knew that he was to build it, that's all.

When the people heard what Noah had to say they wanted to be happy as well. And so, they began to build that ark with Noah, his wife and his children, also.

The ark was designed by the Creator Himself. The dimensions were given carefully to Noah. And the details to which it was to be built were given to Noah in a dream.

Noah was beside himself. He couldn't believe how God was using him. And, as time went on the people from town did stop sinning and did begin to start seeing their need of a Savior. Yes, they remembered about Adam and Eve and about the stories that they had heard about paradise. And, finally they were content and just and righteous.

Time went on and the people from town would build that ark. They loved to hear stories and Noah had so many stories to tell because the Lord God would speak to him almost every night. And when He did, Noah was beside himself.

Noah would tell the stories that he heard to the people, and that would bring them so much joy. And, the joy was so great that their sinning would stop completely.

APPLES AND ORANGES

The children would sit on Noah's lap as he was having lunch and he would tell them about the birds and the bees, and how Eve had taught Adam in the garden of Paradise.

Where the Body Is There the Vultures Gather

And so it was in those days. Noah would continue to build that ark and as he did he continued to teach the children about God and His mighty wisdom. And the children would all learn because they had a thirst and Noah was so interesting to listen to.

The people, on the other hand, were getting tired of this nonsense about a great ark that Noah had told them that God had told

him to build. They became tired, well
because to tell you the truth they did not
have a need for an ark because they lived in
the desert and there are no lakes in the
desert, only sand and rocks and trees.

So the people grew tired of Noah's stories,
too. And one by one they would fall back to
their evil ways, until one day the ark Noah
had built was finished. And on that day
there was a great celebration unlike any
other kind in the forest. And the people
from the town began to have orgies and
drunken parties and they were tempted by
the dark side like they had never been
tempted before. Because this was the day
that our Savior Jesus Christ would come
back and on this day nobody was looking for
Him, only Noah, his wife and his family.

The ark that Noah had built with the help of the town's people was now ready for its voyage. And it was a voyage that we will all have if we are looking toward heaven when Jesus Christ returns.

It's as Close to the Grove as You Can Get

Apples and oranges were to be placed into the ark to prepare Noah and his family for a voyage of a lifetime. It was just beginning to make sense to him. Noah was enlightened, he had free will and he could do as he pleased, but he chose to do God's will and that's the only way that God is going to allow anyone into His kingdom.

CPSIA information can be obtained at www.ICGtesting.com
Printed in the USA
BVOW03*2352010215

385795BV00002B/2/P